IT MIGHT TURN OUT WE ARE REAL

IT MIGHT TURN OUT WE ARE REAL

Susan Scarlata

Horse Less Press

Grateful acknowledgment is given to the following magazines where these poems were first published.

"My Augur, My Backslash" appeared in the Winter 2010 edition of *Typo Magazine*; "To What Do I Most Compare You?," "Married Thinking; Sympathetic Magic," and an earlier version of "Indicators" appeared in the Winter 2010 edition of *Horse Less Review*; "What the Owl Said To Do," "Out of the Eater Came Forth Food," "After the Edict," and "The Eggplant Just Wants to Kill You" appeared in *1913*; and "Phantasmagoria" and "Cure-All" appeared in *Thuggery & Grace*.

Thanks also to Brown University and The University of Denver for time and support. And thank you to my friends, family and teachers for that and more.

© 2011 Susan Scarlata. All rights reserved.

ISBN: 978-0-982989-61-6

Design & typesetting by HR Hegnauer | hrhegnauer.com
Typeset in Cochin.

HORSE LESS PRESS
Denver, Colorado
www.horselesspress.com

PROEM	1
WHAT IS YOUR BUSINESS HERE	2
MESSAGING	3
OF PRTOTYPES AND PAILS	4
OF SEWERS SALES AND SAVINGS	5
THE KEY TO A CIPHER	6
A SET OF ADJACENT BITS USED TO REPRESENT A UNIT OF DATA	7
LAKE OVER A BED OF TIRES	8
PHANTASMAGORIA	9
OF SEWERS AND SALES	10
BEST-LAID	11
DEAL BROKERING	12
WHAT THE OWL SAID TO DO	13
LINES	14
WAIT, DID I MAKE THE UNIVERSE?	15
OUT OF THE EATER CAME FORTH FOOD	16
GOLDEN FLEECE ON THE SUBWAY	17
AFTER THE EDICT	18
OUT OF, CAME FORTH	19
HOW AN ARRANGEMENT MOVES	20
CURE-ALL	21
OF PARTICULAR PLACE OR POSITION	22
TROLLING THE WEB	23
THE VANISHING POINT OF MOTHS	24
MY AUGUR, MY BACKSLASH	25
THE EGGPLANT JUST WANTS TO KILL YOU	26
THE POET, THE POLITICIAN, THE PERFUMER	27
USED TO REPRESENT	28
HOMER, AND SAPPHO, AND FASHION	29
SURE AS A CHILD	30
CLAIRVOYANCE	31
WHAT PART REACHED?	32
VANISHING POINT	33

MARRIED THINKING ... 34
OF ROBOTS AND ALTARS ... 35
FERMENTING WORDS ... 36
SPECIMENS ... 37
A LIVING ... 38
HAPPENING AT THE SAME TIME OR PLACE ... 39
SYMPATHETIC MAGIC ... 40
WHAT PART ... 41
HARD LIVING ... 42
WHAT ADVICE TO TAKE WHEN RAPTURE ... 43
INDICATORS ... 44
SMALL ECONOMIES, OR HOW WE'RE ALL SAVED ... 45
PROMISSORY METAPHOR ... 46
METAPHOR ... 47
CITY MOUSE, COUNTRY MOUSE ... 48
CITY, COUNTRY ... 49
BLUE-LIGHT RACES ... 50
INTELLIGENT DESIGN AND THE ACT OF WRITING ... 51
DESIGN ... 52
SURE AS A CHILD ... 53
OUR MUDDIED HANDS ... 54
OF PELTS AND CUFF-LINKS ... 55
CITIZENS SAVINGS OR THE ORGAN HARVEST ... 56
TO WHAT DO I MOST COMPARE YOU? ... 57
WHAT QUESTIONS TO ASK ... 58
WHAT'S THAT IN YOUR CAR MA'AM? ... 59
WHAT'S THAT? ... 60
WHICH PART WAS OFF? ... 61
QUESTIONS WHEN LEAVING ... 62
PRESCRIBED PATTERN ... 63
DESIRE ... 64
LAST FRAGMENT POEM ... 65

For Jody and all that has come before

PROEM

A recoup of the Sapphic Stanza form, these poems show their cracks, accept their ruin, and get on with it. They are strung, one to the other, linked without attempt to present any sum total. They burgeoned along side investigations of: Ritual sacrifices; Species extinction; Economies of metaphor; Lyric as method of tracing/tracking/absorbing experience; Cyber-spatial identity; Repetition as ritual; and The potentiality of recording. Taking both ancient and contemporary reference and language as lexicons, these poems ply them together, one into the other. They are the interplay, intercourse of ancient principals and contemporary technologies. Old like the lyre and new like the iPad. Old like fire and language thought of as technology, and new like the ever-quickening development of today's devices. Old like form and newer like the field's beyonds. Duration, key to the Sapphic, stands in the background; against the vertigo of speed in our culture, in wonder of our ever-increasing mobility, and continuously changing spatiotemporal conditions. Trying on what is anciently past, what accrues, what reflects on the myriad ways we have reached our varied, current junctions? What possibilities, beyond vanishing (into and out of selves), exist in these times?

WHAT IS YOUR BUSINESS HERE?

I dreamed I carried a snake
to a burnt cracked tree. Then the field
called me doll without saying a word.

    The seat lit on fire

in a pit of burning things.
Do you feel how tatty this has become?
He climbed the mount. He drew the knife.

    The government

says enrich yourself, but leave the
driving to us. Ant noise. Leg shifts.
Then our needs and wants: pollen;

    wool; milk; flax;

reeds to pipe, and a plectrum perhaps;
and we'll call our ship "Ship,"
break nothing on its hull. Here, throw these bits

    in two directions at once.

MESSAGING

Listen, this is how it is. There is
jellyfish thrive, but bees being strangled
and big mammals are hanging out

      at dumpsters.

I am on your machine saying
the micro-chip will release what it holds
only if we cover our

      mirrors, and catch

luminous things on our tongues.
The false prophet is prepared
to offer a thick-legged cow; a

      barren cow; a black cow;

a cow that brought forth but once;
a cow having two colors; and a white barren cow.
When you see us burn things read the smoke

      as what we want.

OF PROTOTYPES AND PAILS

Getting connected with the prototypes
might make this faster, but so far
things remain (the axe to divide the bones;

     several wooden spoons;

and sticks to draw lines around the grounds).
Here is some butter, here is some curd.
If cows are about

     to rain down,

could they wait while we measure the ground?
Build the altar; prepare the vessels;
fetch the food; visit the pump;

     spark the fire; bring the

animal; immolate it and mutter.
Then express the juice; mix the juice
and ferment the juice for 216 hours

     in 720 brass pails.

OF SEWERS SALES AND SAVINGS

Save something already, won't you? We're off
the whales, or off the grid, or the lights are out
tonight, and there are spectrums of

      air for sale, and

every word ever written is getting archived.
You say you are scrubbing
your name from the net like you need

      steel wool to do it.

Meanwhile woodpeckers keep getting what
they want. Repetitive want seems
like a god to me. Let be be

      finale of seem.

The only Emperor lives beneath
the streets where the city foxes retreat.
Leaving their pavement poses,

      their asphalt patience.

THE KEY TO A CIPHER

You lick the corners of your mouth
like the place might flood at any moment.
While astronauts study

dirt on Mars,

people hold pollination contracts up to the light.
Looking for insects,
in pursuit of the bloom, wanting

giant hyssop

or azure sage. Remember
we were bound with willow branches
dipped in the moon to the sacred

stump of a pear tree.

Am I losing you? The white marble
on the altar is stained with blood.
The red behind my ribs is starting to flood.

Wringing out.

ADJACENT BITS USED TO REPRESENT A UNIT OF DATA

Put this sage between two of your vertebrae.
Put this poultice right up against your belly.
Poet write with this balanced

    on your forehead,

and the tree will lean over the cliff
for another thousand years.
From what aspect you ask?

    The future is anywhere

where weeds exist.
The red behind my ribs erodes as
I might hear the bytes. Okay I do, I do

    hear the bytes.

My agapanthus is blue or is white
but is always clustered like
the violets in the lap of she who

    mostly goes astray.

LAKE OVER A BED OF TIRES

Then we crossed the lake of tires.
Two canoes tied together with a shoestring
and the waves began

    to carry us

past the breaker. The water went,
receding so far, when it came back
it would settle scores. For something like this

    we offer

the milk of the goat goddess; the
juice of the creeper plant; the apples
of Iduna; and a mixture of bloods.

    Were we not

prostrate enough? Was my wrist
off? Were my elbows inadequate?
The water came back and wrecked all

    that we had thatched.

PHANTASMAGORIA

That was the time the deity dressed
in the shepherd's gray cloak, and we wore
our lion skins and wolf suits.

    And it was all

Arcadia that whole day long.
If the satyrs are still in the hills,
do you think they are standing and dancing?

    Hoof crunk. To find out

offer a wreath of dandelion pollen
put upon the graves of something scared.
And can you procure that dime bag?

    Can you get us that bong

to put in the poem? And tell me
how are your feet about to plead?
The red behind my ribs is crawling

    back toward what it needs.

OF SEWERS AND SALES

Air for sale.

The magic of

asphalt patience.

BEST-LAID

Will we rent a plot on Hatchet Ranch?
If that girl in the shopping cart
lets go her balloon, we will do

      all we ever intended to.

In the lobby we look over
Meta-verses in the classifieds,
but no other planet meets our needs.

      Plus then

having to friend our avatars,
which is just like so major. Then on
a landline with lacewings, we learn

      we still can't catch our death.

So leave all things staid, the other will be immediate.
Contemporaneous like you shudder
as the blips of bat wings

      fleck the lamplight.

DEAL BROKERING

Deity here is a squash, here is
some sugar cane and melon barely
touched by blight. I am collecting two

      of everything

for when everything gets gone.
Can I order through you? If I
burn the squash and melt the cane each day?

      I can lay out bowls

of milk and saffron, of cinnamon and rice.
Now that I know it was you
that caught the songbirds with your teeth,

      I'm inclined

to say you didn't have to, but I am
so super glad you did. It's off my list
and their songs can help us locate, can lay out

      our intent and territory.

WHAT THE OWL SAID TO DO

The woman, the blend of white owl and person
says we should go get some teeth from a dragon
and sow the teeth to make the next race.

    Did you get that?

Pallas owl, your line broke up.
The bad connection, the static speaking.
What I got was whatever

    as the new whatever.

So we'll write out our favorite words
on slips of clean, bright paper
to burn in the name of whichever

    god we favor.

What if this welter is it? For reals.
What words would you make your own?
The painting on your tongue tells me to start

    the double digging.

LINES

No we could not have been there,
we've been here all day rubbing olive oil
on these rubber plants.

    Plus, we have the longest telecommute.

Alibi ardor. I was wrapped in vellum,
and could barely move.
The CIA redacted me

    from the worldwide web.

I was drunk on aluminum,
reading the bible on ticker tape.
I was putting food on a palm leaf

    in the Ganges.

I could not have been anywhere near there.
I was helping the sea horse
fill its brood pouch

    with eggs.

WAIT, DID I MAKE THE UNIVERSE?

It falls out like mud. The one who threw ashes
up into the sky was, maybe, me?
The stars waxing red, the buckeye

      breaking open.

Your mission is this: to find every living thing
and then to find another,
so to have two of it all, and want

      both the same.

Maybe it *was* always me
who made up the world. Me,
that repealed the apple revoked the egg

      wherever they went.

Now I am looking for my plectrum,
looking for my lyre. I never held a ducat,
but I can image-search

      its picture.

OUT OF THE EATER CAME FORTH FOOD

First is to kill the bull.
Next is to let the flesh lie.
We read this is the way bees are made.

    Lay up many things

to bring forth the bees, but
do not touch the flesh until you hear it loud.
Like behind the red behind the ribs of the bull

    there are angry radio waves.

Pause. Add rosemary to this carcass
maybe a pinch-dash of cardamom.
And when you cannot sleep

    from long waiting,

spatter your face
with the coldest liquid thing,
and listen low and close.

    The hatch will hatch soon.

GOLDEN FLEECE ON THE SUBWAY

People nod off on the train,
content that their soft gold things are safe,
guarded by a dragon that need not sleep.

    At each stop

their hands start and shake, but eyes
only check that the words are not
Hoyt-Schermerhorn, because people like

    to say that. The headlines

of the papers in the peoples' laps
try to exclaim things like "Rampant Recession,"
like "Terror At The Grocery Store!"

    But people are sleeping

on the train. The poet says
the poem should wrap itself around you.
Like that could keep

    anything safe.

AFTER THE EDICT

The night we first heard about getting two
of everything ever, we began
clawing 'tween cushions,

    and we got us some

dusty lint, some inky coins.
You said we could felt them into creatures.
I said they would never sense.

    When we first heard

about getting two of everything,
I felt sure I had heard someone
had done this before.

    The red behind my ribs started

a list of queries. Where are the ice alleys?
How does one splint a paw?
We know not to tourniquet,

    but what if we clot?

OUT OF, CAME FORTH

    Lay

    'til you

    hatch.

HOW AN ARRANGEMENT MOVES

Slugs, you are wetter than shave gel.
Mastodons of humidity,
miracles of disintegration.

      It comes to this:

feed your larva public service announcements;
save your orchids with cinnamon.
We want Adonis' blood

      to turn anemone.

Remember, when we used to keep track
of things by tying knots? I don't really.
But our hands must have got real tired.

      And I bet now

it is harder to touch. Remember
we found that stick shaped just like our highway?
Another way to say this is that

      stuff can re-arrive.

CURE-ALL

The text said meat of honey,
meat of locust you will soon become familiar.
It meant familiar with others like us,

>involved in colonies,

and that meant with bees and with ants.
Then we read that bees gather their babies
in their mouths, which made

>the red behind

my ribs refract light.
The *Eclogues* said they lay inside hides,
and one day burst forth: bees over clover.

>We offered sage,

the pectin in quince, and frankincense and stuff
to make the most feral apiary ever.
To make it seem simple

>to cultivate their adaptations.

OF PARTICULAR PLACE OR POSITION

I was in this wool sweater,
or I was in sea water, up to my neck
sucking salt through my sinuses.

    Then behind my ribs

my dream split in two.
In one we were eating off maps
in the other prisms were breaking light,

    and the hues were telling me what to do.

And there is something I keep meaning to tell you.
I have too much to text you.
It's that in order to fragment

    we should separate,

filter off, cull, flush out what we can.
The alphabet behind my spine,
feeling around for sharp edges, knows

    all this too well.

TROLLING THE WEB

Tiny red 'x' closes things out.
Deer splay on the highway,
and we say pull it up, and mean the green plus.

    I think chat rooms

must have the slight furniture,
and are most like basements with false ceilings.
And in these spaces trolls abound

    with their caustic pools of words,

but a good-codes-witch exists
who makes ways to dis-emvowel them.
Each chat surrounded by perimeter of magnets,

    that pull vowels out

of paragraphs, sentences, words.
Then there they are. Primitive alphabets.
Pressing consonant to consonant,

    throats with no mouths.

THE VANISHING POINT OF MOTHS

Curtains, if recognized patterns block
pornos from YouTube, whose soft hands are those
tying anise stems together? And where are my

    gold anklebone cuffs when I need them?

This winter, wool-holes the size of moth mouths.
Body marking. Tell me curtains,
if most often it is the erotic that sets things

    in motion,

how do dragonflies converge? And
how much fat can a black bear get
eating a cluster of moths? The poets

    write "moth dust" and "wing light,"

but flies ground into carpet too.
And how 'bout hollow cloud? Shallow cloud?
Where what we muster

    is all about what we can take.

MY AUGUR, MY BACKSLASH

Poaching this slow connection,
I read that my avatar screwed around with my augur.
While the machine is

    always saying: You

cannot connect this. Someone
left their malt out by the pay phone,
and we stop and think, some body's moon.

    Curb wreck, bumper rub.

We dream of long boar teeth,
so the red behind my ribs is stacking itself
to climb away. But we will have

    to have a boar in this,

so posthumously people can float
the term "heroic," about us,
so my avatar can go down as

    loose with soothsayers.

THE EGGPLANT JUST WANTS TO KILL YOU

How many persimmons equal an elephant?
Haggling over representation. Tusk love.
While people round up feral cats at the airport,

    have you noticed

a resurgence of astronauts?
Astronaut on the cereal box and astronauts
dancing as stars? They are everywhere

    I read. The one poet

says give me your thee. While
the other poet's eyes are all over.
And my cell phone sounds like a rap song,

    and my rap song sounds

like a washer up in arms.
The text says when the nightshades show up
they want to kill you, while our hard-drives hold

    all our cut words "in mind."

THE POET, THE POLITICIAN, THE PERFUMERS

The poet says her teeth have sexual problems.
I say teeth are shells telling us where we are.
That all our tongues are camouflaged

      cephalopods.

The politician distractedly says
"It's all a distraction," and just then
my ISP begins to hate my server.

      So what

are those depending on other planets to do
when the fear of loosestrife takes over?
When animals cum generalists

      surround us? We'll just

put our tongues together, taste the smells
we've wanted for: honeysuckle, myrtle, heliotrope.
See if purple has its own waft. Sorry, better dash

      my screen just woke up.

USED TO REPRESENT

Your

future is anywhere

the bytes

go astray.

HOMER AND SAPPHO AND FASHION

When people heard our plans
it was like we got popular,
and they listened and looked

    at us different.

It goes back to how Homer wrote
that at the end of that one big fight
all the women were "beating their chests,

    clinging to the statues of heroes,"

so the men had to peel them down.
And it has to do with these days how
women can be dumpster chic or drunkorexia,

    or demented chic.

And after Homer Sappho wrote
"strike yourselves girls and tear your garments
'til you are," and she tore, and

    and was ecstatically bare.

SURE AS A CHILD

The children think everyone is thinking
what they are thinking until
they realize different.

      One blots her tears

with a balled up sock.
The other keeps talking with the decapede.
They all tell each other "that happened

      before you were born."

And when they see a puppet,
and the hand inside the puppet
asks what it means if the puppet dies

      the kids agree that

it would mean no more puppet body,
but that the puppet would still feel.
Then out the window, the glory

      squirrel was twirl!

CLAIRVOYANCE

Dear squirrel, I know you
were in my kitchen again.
You left your favorite daisies

    all over the floor.

Squirrel, are you fey? Would you tell me
if you were? I heard the mason bee
goes solo. Laying eggs in cavities.

    How 'bout you?

Where is your web-enabled-mobile-device?
Do you feel for multi-touch technology,
or want more blue

    jacaranda?

Your daises smell of hibiscus or blood.
What say you, squirrel?
Do you mean to spill your teeth

    as you float out my window?

WHAT PART REACHED?

Phone, have you climbed behind my ribs yet?
I hear your re-mixed ring. Printer crunch.
Fax bleat. Like magic cabinets get filled

      with early adopters.

In the long-distance relationship
the phone lines fleet.
In the short-distance relationship

      lines of the poem on the street.

Either way, our atmosphere with its thickening skin.
Listen, words were once carved on wax tablets
then placed in jars for safe keeping.

      And what's strange about

the hippocampus is how it's both
a sea creature of whimsy, part fish and part horse;
and the ridged part of our brains where our

      shortest of memories spend time.

VANISHING POINT

    When I need

    things in motion.

    Wing light

    it is.

MARRIED THINKING

He said over my head like it was under my chin,
and meant out of my league
with no inclination that

    one of these clichés

referenced the body.
She said the mark the sheets leave on your teeth,
or there is something between your cheeks.

    When wings began

to erupt from his elbows
she said, "I always thought your unborn twin
would come from your throat."

    He said something

about mitochondria, that it was
mitosis not meiosis,
but she could not tell the difference

    any longer.

OF ROBOTS AND ALTARS

Hello washing machine, is that your book
about when robots take the world?
I glanced at it, and began to feel

      the shivering wings

of plague-ridden insects. Then guessed
I should be making an altar. Supple, sacrosanct.
For after we bludgeon the ox,

      I read it or

felt it somewhere. Tableaus of tabernacles.
We give the flesh of the ox lavender-laced branches.
We surround it all with grass

      and fire

on which we'll tromp and tramp.
So listen future-cyborg, I need these
bloody garments washed, so later

      I can tear them.

FERMENTING WORDS

Express the juice, dilute the juice with water;
mix it with barley meal;
clarified butter; and

    some peat from the bog;

then ferment it for nine days in a jar.
Like words. Speaking we use
fewer words than we read, and writing

    we use fewer

words than we speak. Do we
feel a point? Sometimes we feel a point.
Teenagers in want of consistence

    snap the match, striking it off

the zippers of their skinny jeans.
But fire is not consistency,
fire is just fire even if sometimes

    it crawls through the brush.

SPECIMENS

The ones caught, stuffed, and taxonimied
are covered over in arsenic.
While the live ones keep adapting to our habits.

     Seagulls swoop through

super market parking lot in a landlocked state
where it's too mild to migrate.
The factory-farmed cow stands bloated

     full of plastic capsules.

And if we drug our cows, which indeed we do.
If you eat a clone
how much clone does that make you?

     Ruminants without cud.

Their jaws are sore, I feel it.
We need alfalfa! Leaves of Grass!
A heifer making nectar

     beneath a low-flung moon.

A LIVING

Pollination events exist
because there are people pimping bees.
Even the oldest profession

        has been hit by recession.

But still the old man wants a French Job.
The honey the bees made from almond flowers was
too bitter to eat. And the cows of two colors stayed

        drugged 'til death.

My psoas is in knots, my back-body shaping
the next thing to come is
yarrow root. To balance the flora

        in your gut.

And the sun promotes the giving
while the clouds promote the taking.
It's our operating system,

        our external drive.

HAPPENING AT THE SAME TIME OR PLACE

The bees will hatch from within the dying skin.
The red behind my ribs becomes
a hater, but then others

      tell it too.

Like "he returned to take her,
and there found the carcass of
a lion, and within found bees with

      their combs in

the carcass of the lion."
Be ever aware that this happened
on some ship. That seeing these bees

      he did not rape her.

Shit we might think, magic does happen.
In thanks we might offer minerals from the fat
of three sea mammals, the twisted part of a narwhal, maybe

      some gold-plated chickpeas.

SYMPATHETIC MAGIC

Within a closed chest we are
growing fennel, lettuce,
and other shallow-rooted things

      on every flat roof

    while pigeons on our turrets gather and prune.
It is getting clearer with time:
if I swept the window sills the

      Iraqui Oud player in exile

voted for Obama.
That I'm saying that I'm frangible,
palming this difference.

      Toothing cuticles,

rubbing my fists with eyes. A child learning
to snap, a tree starting to sap. Screw it
no matter what happens, on the eighth day we hurl

      the greenery to the sea.

WHAT

Poems on the street.

The strangest

spent time.

HARD LIVING

In your gut

is never external.

WHAT ADVICE TO TAKE, WHEN RAPTURE

Ceiling fan, with micro genres and
teeny niches will we ever reach each other?
Is my email's advice to:

    "Be safe and be smart"

actual? And if rapture
pray tell, will bacteria brought
over by the immigrant truly

    rejuvenate the trauma-dome?

And disaster, what did you say
at your caucus? How many make up
your quorum? Marketers

    troll for places

where people are most captive. Coping like weeds,
copping their feel. The code will be
the one thing that does not repeat

    between the radio's waves.

INDICATORS

Oh jellyfish you are ever-where.
And dear white bears,
you can barely hear our carburetors

      melting the ice caps.

Beyond bituminous humus it is thistle
and loosestrife that like what people do.
Thistle grasps whatever ground like a needle sucks.

      Jellyfish, is it

your lack of brain, or heart, or bones
that accounts for how you love what we do?
You wouldn't get it, how we're making the garden

      not to fruit, but to remember

succession, the fragments we possibly occupy;
to call up the one born when the tusks of the boar did rend
the bark of a myrrh tree. By accident we are fashioning this

      for you, dear weeds, to inherit.

SMALL ECONOMIES, OR HOW WE'RE ALL SAVED

The gristle was laid up in the treasury.
Some of the spoils were laid up,
others were melted down and

      dispersed.

The first fruits were cut up and laid up,
but the fruit was the seed or the fruit was the stem
marked as a line item in the books.

      The temple, the vault is

full up with these notes. Promissory metaphors.
Commercial paper. Like the image was
concealed in a bundle of baked liver,

      or a bunch of sticks

bound together, or a package
of iron rods bound to one another,
or in the tight pockets of a couple

      of fags making out.

PROMISSORY METAPHOR

To cause the blood to flow,
use the splinter of stone which is white,
or the oval-shaped rock which is jet.

    Kill the elephant

with the smallest arrow you have.
This is my bronze shiv, my obsidian knife.
It is human to say, "The better to eat you with."

    To cause obscene scene,

use this slit of volcanic glass.
The red bead was drawn from her throat,
but she was saved by being wrapped in a cloud.

    Today the sky is

clear for miles. I had my people lay up
the shells, the gems, the stones: all preciousness;
and make votives out of words, knowing language

    will fill its own holes.

METAPHOR

The elephant

caused a scene.

The sky

filled its holes.

CITY MOUSE, COUNTRY MOUSE

Stranger don't worry, I don't think you're alone.
You can put your phone down,
look around. There's squirrel perch and

    pigeon chest.

Jutting off fire escapes, pecking on chimneys,
feeling across phone wires. The poet wrote
"When you call your brother on the phone it is holy."

    I have never had a brother.

Stranger, we are in this together
hearing the same colors
feeling the same machines.

    The computing cloud

does not know what we want, it's just so good at
pretending, making the sky something technical.
No I am not writing a letter, this is *not* an outline.

    Look, it's squirrel curl and pigeon slump.

COUNTRY, CITY

    Pigeon chest

    I never had

    pigeon slump.

BLUE-LIGHT RACES

Trained to click over linked things we can't
if too much nitrogen in the soil
makes the broccoli leaf and not fruit.

    And we can't without feeding the fire first.

We will give a dwarf ox, a drooping-horned bull,
a piebald ox, a white ox, and a mule
all for that car called Cayenne.

    I have the spit,

the spoons, the pots, the grass;
but our offer today became a
blue-light-special and people

    trampled the doorman

to be the first to get at it. Oh apple
in the big market, you are so conventional.
Where is the millet-seed, the

    citizen's grain?

INTELLIGENT DESIGN AND THE ACT OF WRITING

Parthenogenesis plays opposite
the sea horse's brood pouch,
or the penguins' gestation period.

      The female Komodo

Dragon can make it happen without sperm,
but must be under duress.
And then slugs with

      all their organs, and

slugs with all their members.
And after the affair one castrates the other
with whatever slug mouth they have.

      Is there a struggle?

Or is it set in the act? They will not say,
but their sex is a perfect spiral
bound notebook in which poets keep writing

      eggs, lines, sperms.

DESIGN

The female

has organs.

Has eggs and lines,

but no.

SURE AS A CHILD

Blot her tears with

for you were born.

OUR MUDDIED HANDS

Trying to yield Lily of the Valley,
we want a little somethin' somethin'
for every deity. As loud as we can

      we shout turn off the century!

But no one can reach that switch. So we know
somewhere the smoke of sacrifice rises with
no one around to read into it. We look down and

      our hands are covered over in oil.

It will take so much to cut this.
How much fat of the olive leaf
to break this tint and stain?

      Where are the bone-bright beaches?

To fix all this will take so much of us,
could set us back to Precambria.
Fetch some flax and whites of eggs.

      Use the wolfsbane salve.

OF PELTS AND CUFF-LINKS

The surveillance video was a junk-show.
But this pelt's for you, and you'd look sharp
in the wolf-suit too.

    Kiss your cuff-links,

do whatever else it is that you do to prepare.
We are burning tufts of wool,
cashmere yak hair, and some tailings

    from the slag piles by the highway.

The metal we wanted in the ore was near
the rabbit running away proves
leaving is always acrobatics.

    Fire, our offer is ghee,

so you will keep flaring, ad infinitum.
Broom, we ask that you don't lose your straw.
We're not ready for the implications of

    such suchness.

CITIZENS SAVINGS OR THE ORGAN HARVEST

Our monoculture makes for brittle systems.
We always want the one that got away.
We have our seed vaults with

        vacuum seals

at constant cold temperatures,
our cats and dogs cryogenically on ice.
All the epithelium, every gizzard we could get,

        sitting in this silo.

While the red behind my ribs slithers
through my trunk, my epiglottis got caught
in something viscous, reluctant to flow.

        And you with your brand new

esophagus? Did you know all these
secondhand organs are only allowed
to go in bodies whose mouths swear

        they will behave?

TO WHAT DO I MOST COMPARE YOU?

The image of man, not the man himself.
We tie you to the post,
but let you go, 'cause God is

    not a metaphor.

We know, we know, the knife was blunt
the ram caught in thicket, or a deer appears,
"in the place of," or

    it's just a bead of blood

that will suffice. Synecdochic day.
Part for the whole, and "civilized" starts.
Just the grizzle from the fat. Stand-in.

    Just how butter smells,

just the lamb damage, ox crash, busted bull.
You know that we know, it's birds caught in propellers,
or how either side of the metaphor can do in

    what it's compared to.

WHAT QUESTIONS TO ASK

I was bleeding against the moon,
not when it is sloughing off,
when the hive started happening.

The carcass became locus.

Base. We kept returning to check
then because we were there
we started asking the carcass questions.

Looking to interpret any sign

that could be an answer.
What's bona fide? Who is tangible enough
to be valid? Behind my ribs, the red

assessing what we have

been through. How are the pachyderms faring?
Have the dragon's teeth spawned?
Have we thanked the periphrastic phrase,

or yet traced the right face?

WHAT'S THAT IN YOUR CAR MA'AM?

More questions for our augur, our oracular corpse:
Can we change the stream mid course?
What does the flight pattern of the pelican

    propitiate?

We want to come close in un-bloody ways.
We split this offer in three equal parts.
For us, for them and

    for those that ain't got any.

The offer is a goat or it is a camel,
and it must be healthy and conscious, alive.
We are in the car again with

    some mammal that is lowing.

We pass a pay phone and think
they still exist,
and the creature's lowing is getting louder,

    like capture.

WHAT'S THAT

Propitiate?

WHICH PART WAS OFF?

After the cyclone comes an earthquake,
and we sit back and wonder
was it not enough jasmine?

    Do we need more

trace tastes of marjoram? The one thing
for sure, our ritual is fucked.
Did we bury all the books

    before the torrent?

Whose outburst is this?
Should we hold a serious séance?
Do we need to call back the harpies?

    The tastemaker behind my ribs

eyes the insects on barbed wire. Skims
Vimeos for a face of God. Unearthed things
muddy and ruined. Empty hands still poised to hold

    whatever they were trying to save.

QUESTIONS WHEN LEAVING

Dear Swallow, I will never get when you gag,
but I know when the red
behind my ribs hydroplanes.

    Nothing touching.

Swallow, is it reflex
like swans tuck their necks in their backs,
or more linked to video-sharing portals?

    We saw those all over

the road. When we found goose wreck
all we could know was gods like caverns,
we might slip into, and God to be believed

    when he speaks of his gun.

Do we go anyway?
If the fissure gets bigger, do we go
inland, or close to the coast?

    What is it we're after?

PRESCRIBED PATTERNS

I was told about Afghani poppy crops,
about beetles that feed on ambrosia.
Told to lay the fish's liver on

      hot coals.

I was told to paint the horses with dreams,
to offer young lambs by torchlight.
I was told what

      could avalanche.

Was told to protect the image, whether
in bundle, or willow, or pocket.
Told to votive whatever while unplugging the field.

      Now in flash of elk-butt white

we are about to lay up,
to paint, to offer the golden tumor
out of the belly of

      the beast.

PRAYER

It was a machine that asked, "Did you really think
you could scan our reverse zones?"
Which told us something (though what

      I am not sure) about pulling

ourselves together. For the well planned mash-up,
the elephant carrying astronauts,
that their spines become the ridge lines.

      Hear it. For the army

of aubergine plants, the bees
being born out of lions. Hear it. That that
one frog keeps throwing up its offspring. Hear it.

      That no one uploads

this moth dust or downloads that bear strut.
Hear it. That we use our intricate moves for
something with succor. Hear it. The poet says, "West,"

      and beyond a white field's a white sky.

LAST FRAGMENT

What

prayer

can learn

beyond a white field.

NOTES

IT MIGHT TURN OUT WE ARE REAL

The title first appeared in the book *You Are Not A Gadget* by Jaron Lanier.

WHAT IS YOUR BUSINESS HERE?

"He climbed the mount/He drew the knife" references Abraham in the parable where God tests his belief by asking him to sacrifice his son Isaac. On the way up "Isaac asks Abraham where the lamb is for the burnt offering, and Abraham says, God will provide Himself the lamb for the burnt offering, my son" (Kierkegaard's *Fear and Trembling*). A ram appears in the thicket at the last moment to be used as a stand-in sacrifice. This story appears in *The Book of Genesis*, 22:2-23 as well as in the Koran.

"Enrich yourselves, but leave the driving to us," is a direct quote from a political pamphlet designed by the Communist Party in China.

A plectrum is a spear point used for striking the lyre, the Latinized form of the Greek (pléktron).

MESSAGING

The "bees being strangled" refers to a syndrome currently affecting many bee colonies known as *Colony Collapse Disorder (CCD)*. Also called *Disappearing Disease, Spring Dwindle, May disease, Autumn Collapse, Honey Bee Depopulation Syndrome* and *Fall Dwindle*

Disease, it was first reported in 2006 in North America. Since then colonies in at least twenty-four U.S. states, and many other countries have reported similar syndromes. Affected hives have worker bees that leave and never come back. There are many theories as to causes: cell phones; pesticides; pests; and viruses; but there is not yet any definitive diagnosis. Some consider CCD to be the insect equivalent of AIDS as it affects bees' immune systems. Between the 1970s and today, feral bee populations have become virtually non-existent due to industrial agriculture and human encroachment on wild lands. Beekeepers transport their "commercial" bees from coast to coast as various crops need to be pollinated. From almonds in California to blueberries in Maine, people shuttle their bees across the country all year long. Having become so transient, area-specific adaptations and tolerances no longer exist in these bee colonies.

The various descriptions of cows in this poem come from the Hindu *Vedas*.

OF PROTOTYPES AND PAILS

The list of tasks is borrowed from the Hindu *Vedas*.

OF SEWERS SALES AND SAVINGS

"Repetitive want seems like a god to me" is a reference to the line, "he seems to me equal to gods that man," from Sappho's *Fragment 31* (*If Not Winter*, Carson).

"Let be be/finale of/ seem The only Emperor" is a direct quote from Wallace Stevens' poem *The Emperor of Ice-Cream.*

THE KEY TO A CIPHER

"Remember we/were bound with willow-sticks full of lunar magic to the sacred," comes from Ernest Cushing Richardson's *Beginning of Libraries*.

A SET OF ADJACENT BITS USED TO REPRESENT A UNIT OF DATA

An agapanthus is a blue or purple flower also known as "The Lily of the Nile."

Sappho's *Fragment 21* contains the lines "the one with violets in her lap/]mostly/]goes astray" (*If Not Winter*, Carson).

LAKE OVER A BED OF TIRES

"For something like this we offer…" is from the Hindu *Vedas*.

PHANTASMAGORIA

Arcadia is a region of southern Greece and has historically represented an idealized rustic paradise in literature.

In Greek mythology satyrs are a class of lustful woodland gods pictured as men with goat's ears, tail, legs and horns.

Crunk is a type of frenetic, urban, contemporary music and dance that fuses elements of hip-hop and electronica.

BEST-LAID

Avatar is a Sanskrit word for "a form of self," which in Hinduism is used as a term for an incarnation of a divinity. This word has recently grown in popularity with the contemporary meaning of "digital persona." Digital avatars are used in online games or business as electronic representations of an individual's public personality or, alternately, what a person might like their personality to be.

WHAT THE OWL SAID TO DO

The woman/owl refers to the Greek Goddess Pallas Athena. In some versions of the Greek myth about Jason, the Argonauts and their attempt to retrieve the Golden Fleece, it is Athena who tells Jason to "sow the teeth of dragons," which created the first sons of Thebes.

In Venezuela and other countries it is tradition to write wishes on slips of paper and burn them on New Years Eve each year.

Double digging is a sustainable farming practice that aerates the deeper layers of a garden's soil in order to improve drainage and help roots thrive.

LINES

"Rubbing olive/oil on these rubber plants," is a direct quote from Alfred Hitchcock's *Vertigo*. The lines are uttered at the Inn when Jimmy Stewart has watched Kim Novak enter and disappear. The woman behind the hotel counter says that no one has passed through. I would know, she says, I've been here all day "Rubbing olive/oil on these rubber plants."

"Putting/food on a palm /leaf in the Ganges," is a tradition, among many others, performed as a part of the Hindu holiday Diwali or "festival of lights." It symbolizes the lifting of spiritual darkness and marks the beginning of the Hindu New Year.

In sea horses the male of the species becomes pregnant; eggs are fertilized and hatch in the male's brood pouch.

WAIT, DID I MAKE THE UNIVERSE?

"It falls out like mud" is a direct quote from the definition for *Bitumen (a shellfish)* in *Aztec Definitions* in *Technicians of the Sacred* edited by Jerome Rothenberg.

A Ducat is a gold coin formerly used in Europe.

OUT OF THE EATER CAME FORTH FOOD

The title of this poem comes from *The Book of Judges* 14:14.

"First is to kill the bull/Next is…" is a reference to Virgil's *Autogenesis of Bees* in the *Eclogues* (Bk IV: 281-314), an explanation of ways that bees are made.

GOLDEN FLEECE ON THE SUBWAY

Hoyt-Schermerhorn is a subway stop in Brooklyn Heights, NY.

The un-sleeping Dragon appears in the myth of Jason and the Argonauts, as the being charged with guarding the Golden Fleece, making it more difficult for Jason to retrieve the fleece.

The poet who said that "the poem should wrap itself around you," is Frank O'Hara.

HOW AN ARRANGEMENT MOVES

Remember when we used to keep/track of things by tying knots appears in Ernest Cushing Richardson's *The Beginning of Libraries* as an early form of writing.

"We want Adonis'/blood to anemone" is related to the myth of Adonis' love affair with Aphrodite. The two lovers often hunted together in the woods. Adonis chased game and Aphrodite would follow closely behind, in her swan-driven chariot. Aphrodite's ex-lover, Ares, grew jealous of her affair with this mortal. While Adonis was hunting alone, Ares disguised himself as a boar and attacked Adonis causing him lethal injuries. Adonis struck back, but was soon gored to death by the boar's great tusks. Aphrodite hurried to Adonis, but his soul had already descended into the Underworld. In despair, she sprinkled nectar on Adonis' wounds, and as she carried her lover's body out of the woods, crimson anemones sprung up where each drop of blood fell on the earth.

CURE-ALL

"The text said meat of honey meat/of locust" is a reference to John the Baptist from the Bible's *Book of Matthew* 3:4.

TROLLING THE WEB

Refers to people designated as Internet trolls who participate in Internet chat rooms just to ridicule and deceive other people. Programmers have developed ways to detect trolls through attributes of their writing. Once recognized, they have developed codes that "dis-emvowel," or extract all the vowels from what a troll writes, rendering it into gibberish.

In primitive alphabets the world-over shifts toward greater freedom of expression and eventual literacy took place when vowels were introduced in to alphabets. Before vowels were introduced, creating space within words, languages were made up entirely of consonants.

THE VANISHING POINT OF MOTHS

In its initial years the creators of *YouTube* made a conscious choice not to allow people to post pornographic videos to their site. Many technological innovations begin in the porn industry because there is significant, continuous demand. *YouTube's* creators realized that if they allowed porn, their site would quickly become nothing but that. So, similarly to codes that attempt to block trolls, *YouTube* has codes that recognize patterns, which alert the site to potentially pornographic content.

"Whose soft / hands are tying the anise stems," is an inversion of a line that appears in Sappho's *Fragment 81* (*If Not Winter*, Carson).

THE EGGPLANT JUST WANTS TO KILL YOU

This is a personal anecdote from a friend who was seeing a Naturopath. He was told that he should avoid eating all plants of the Nightshade family, including eggplants because, in all seriousness "Nightshades just want to kill you."

The poet saying "give me your thee" is Robert Duncan, the other poet, whose "eyes are everywhere" is Louis Zukofsky.

THE POET, THE POLITICIAN, THE PERFUMER

The poet who says her "teeth have sex-/ual problems" is Bernadette Mayer.

An ISP is an Internet service provider.

Heliotropes are deep purple flowers that smell like vanilla, also called "turnsole," because its flowers and leaves turn toward the sun over the course of each day. At night the plant readjusts itself to face eastward, to be ready for sunrise. That is where the word heliotrope comes from too, meaning to move with the sun.

Cephalopods are an underwater species including octopuses, squid, cuttlefish and nautiluses. They can change color, texture and body shape to camouflage themselves and also "disappear" in a cloud of ink.

HOMER AND SAPPHO AND FASHION

All the women "beating their/chests clinging to the statues of/ heroes," is an image that appears at the end of Homer's *Iliad*.

"Dumpster/chic" and "Demented chic," are both terms used for current styles of women's fashion that appeared in *T,* the Fashion Supplement of the *New York Times*.

Drunkorexia is a slang term that describes the practice of restricting one's food intake in order to drink more alcohol, and sustain oneself on the calories from alcohol alone.

In *Fragment 140* Sappho wrote, "delicate Adonis is dying/ Kythereia /what should we do? /strike yourselves/ maidens /

and tear your garments" (*If Not, Winter* Carson). This fragment demonstrates Sappho's supposed participation in the *Cult of Adonis*.

MARRIED THINKNG

Mitosis is a process of cell division that results in the production of two daughter cells from a single parent cell. The daughter cells are identical to one another and to the original parent cell. Meiosis is the type of cell division by which germ cells (eggs and sperm) are produced. Meiosis involves a reduction in the amount of genetic material, comprising two successive nuclear divisions with only one round of DNA replication.

OF ROBOTS AND ALTARS

"Shivering wings" refers to one of the symptoms of *Colony Collapse Disorder* where bees cannot stop their wings from shaking.

Tearing garments is a part of the Cult of Adonis ritual (see notes for *Homer and Sappho and Fashion Week*).

FERMENTING WORDS

The ritual detailed in this poem ("express the juice" etc.) comes from the Hindu *Vedas*.

Fermenting words in jars comes from Richardson's *Beginning of Libraries*, as another primordial word-related ritual.

SPECIMENS

The cow's soar jaw refers to the fact that in many Factory Farms cows are fed corn products. Eating corn cows do not need to chew intensely and then regurgitate as they must when eating greens, roughage and other grains. Their ruminant stomachs and cud-chewing mouths and jaws are made to digest roughage, so corn-fed cows are eternally ill, and must be pumped full of antibiotics.

A LIVING

Refers to a study that demonstrated that people steal more and commit more crimes in general when the sun is not out than when it is.

HAPPENING AT THE SAME TIME OR PLACE

"He returned to take her/and there found the carcass of a/lion and within found bees with/their combs in the/carcass of the lion" is a direct quote from *The Book of Judges* 14:8.

In Sappho's *Fragment 143* "gold chickpeas were growing on the banks."

SYMPATHETIC MAGIC

"Adonis' closed chest" refers to Adonis, the annually renewed, ever-youthful vegetation god; a life-death-rebirth deity. The chest is the box in which Adonis was sent as a baby from Aphrodite to Persephone in order to hide his great beauty. When Adonis grows up he becomes Aphrodite's lover and is killed by a boar while out hunting one day. Aphrodite then pleads with Zeus to bring Adonis back to life. Zeus agrees, but with the understanding that Adonis has to stay in the underworld during winter and be with Aphrodite only in summer, thus vegetation dies in winter and blossoms in summer.

Women in the Cult of Adonis celebrated in the spring with great joy and took part in mourning festivals in the winter. They planted gardens of Adonis including fennel, lettuce and other plants with shallow roots. They grew these plants, watering with warm water in chests, on flat roofs, and in sherds and shards for eight days. And on the eighth day they would "hurl the/greenery to the sea," marking Adonis' short life and the general ephemeral state of living.

An Iraqui who was given asylum in the United States due to his Oud-playing abilities was interviewed on the radio after the 2008 U.S. Presidential election during which he announced whom he voted for.

WHAT ADVICE TO TAKE WHEN RAPTURE

On the sign-in page of a University email account I once had it truly stated "Be safe and be smart."

"Bacteria / carried by the immigrant / rejuvenate / the trauma-dome" appeared on the *Action Books* website for a number of years.

Historically codes issued through radio waves were the bits that did not repeat amongst all the sounds being issued.

INDICATORS

Ironically, the plant and animal species considered to be pests to humans flourish in the areas most affected by environmental degradations: jellyfish, plants we have taken to calling weeds and all adaptable generalists thrive in unwelcoming, extremely warm climates.

Adonis gardens were purposely un-useful and ephemeral, planted not for sustenance but for their imagery and symbolism.

Adonis was said to have been born "when the boars'/tusks did rend the bark of a myrrh tree." This connects with his death when attacked by a boar. Women in the cult of Adonis "plant[ed] pleasant plants," they "sow[ed] in sherds and shards."

SMALL ECONOMIES, OR HOW WE'RE ALL SAVED

The gristle laid up comes from myths related to Prometheus. Having been forbidden to help humans, Prometheus helps them anyway, guiding them in a matter of division of sacrifice. Prometheus divides an ox into two piles; in one he puts all the meat and most of the fat, covering it with the ox's stomach, while in the other pile, he dresses up the bones with shining fat. Prometheus then invites Zeus to choose a pile for the gods. This provides an explanation for the common practice in ancient Greece where worshipers sacrificed only bones to the gods, while keeping the meat and fat for themselves. When Zeus realized he had been tricked he denied humankind the secret of fire. Prometheus could not bear seeing humans suffering in the cold and stole fire from the hearth of the gods and brought it to the humans. Fire can be seen as the very first "technology" that humans had to use. When Zeus discovered Prometheus' further transgression he condemned him to be chained to a rock where birds would peck at his liver every day, and his liver would regenerate at night, unto eternity.

"Promissory/metaphors" are all of the objects, fruits of labor, and spoils of war listed in the registries of temples as things offered to gods while being used by humans in their earthly lives.

"Baked liver," "bundles of sticks," and "packages of iron rods," are all things that have been defined as "faggots" at some point in history.

PROMISSORY METAPHOR

"The better to eat you with," is a reference to the image we have made of the Wolf in the *Little Red Riding Hood* fairy tale.

"The /bead drawn from the throat," references the bead of blood offered instead of Iphigenia's life in the story of she and her father, Agamemnon. As the leader of the Greek forces at Troy, Agamemnon was ordered to sacrifice his daughter to appease Artemis. Agamemnon had offended Artemis, the virgin goddess of the hunt, by killing one of her sacred animals. Artemis sent a contrary wind, which held the Greek fleet in the bay of Aulis, where it had assembled before sailing to Troy. The prophet Calchas divined that the daughter of Agamemnon would have to be sacrificed to atone for the offence. Agamemnon then summoned Iphigenia under the ruse that she was to be married to Achilles. Different versions vary the ending of this myth. In some a bead of Iphigenia's blood is offered instead of her life, in others she is miraculously transported to a city on the Black Sea, and an animal is sent in her place. In still other versions Iphigenia is actually sacrificed.

CITY MOUSE, COUNTRY MOUSE

The title of this poem refers to the children's story, *City Mouse and Country Mouse* written and illustrated by Isabelle Chantellard.

The poet that wrote "When you/call your brother on the phone it/is holy," is Jack Spicer.

BLUE-LIGHT RACES

The un-fed fire references the Hindu tradition of keeping a flame going for a lifetime as the fire itself is the essence of the god Agni.

The list of various oxen and mules comes from the Hindu *Vedas*.

The "trampled doorman" refers to the "doorkeeper" whose feet are "seven armlengths long," in Sappho's *110th Fragment*, and also to the person opening a Wal-Mart on Black Friday of 2008 who was trampled by people pushing and shoving to get to be the first ones in.

Produce not grown using organic methods is commonly referred to as "conventional," so the type of farming that uses pesticides and other chemicals has become the standard.

"Millet seed/of the citizen" comes directly from Sappho's *Fragment 5*.

INTELLIGENT DESIGN AND THE ACT OF WRITING

The "theory" of Intelligent Design holds that certain features of the universe and of living things are best explained by an intelligent cause, not an "undirected process" such as natural selection.

Parthenogenesis literally translates to "virgin birth" (from the Greek, "parthen" meaning virgin or maiden and "genesis" meaning beginning.

Female Komodo Dragons will sometimes use a form of virgin birth where it hatches eggs without conception. Biological cloning is not a recent scientific invention, but an ancient ability various species have utilized as a stopgap when there are no appropriate mates in their vicinity.

Slugs have both male and female organs until they have sex after which one castrates the other.

www.ingramcontent.com/pod-product-compliance
Lightning Source LLC
Chambersburg PA
CBHW031207090426
42736CB00009B/812